Abby Wambach

By Jon M. Fishman

AMAZING ATHLETES

Lerner Publications Company • Minneapolis

Lerner Publications Company
A division of Lerner Publishing Group, Inc.
241 First Avenue North
Minneapolis, MN 55401 USA

For reading levels and more information, look up this title at www.lernerbooks.com.

Library of Congress Cataloging-in-Publication Data

Fishman, Jon M.
    Abby Wambach / by Jon M. Fishman.
        pages   cm. — (Amazing athletes)
    Includes index.
    ISBN 978–1–4677–2141–7 (lib. bdg. : alk. paper)
    ISBN 978–1–4677–2436–4 (eBook)
    1. Wambach, Abby, 1980– 2. Women soccer players—United States—Biography—Juvenile literature. 3. Soccer players—United States—Biography—Juvenile literature. I. Title.
GV942.7.W36F57 2014
796.334092—dc23 [B]   2013022665

Manufactured in the United States of America
1 – BP – 12/31/13

TABLE OF CONTENTS

Abby Wambach *(front right)* tries to score a goal against Canada.

A CHANCE FOR GOLD

Abby Wambach and her teammates were struggling. The US Women's National Team trailed the Canada Women's National Team by one goal, 3–2. They were playing in a **semifinal** match at the 2012 Olympic Games in London, England. The winner would go on to play in the gold medal match a few days later.

It's hard to score goals in soccer. Many soccer matches end with just one or two balls in the nets. But Team USA had already scored twice. Abby knew they could do it again and tie the game. "Even when they scored their third goal, there was something in me that knew that we had more, that we could give more," Abby said.

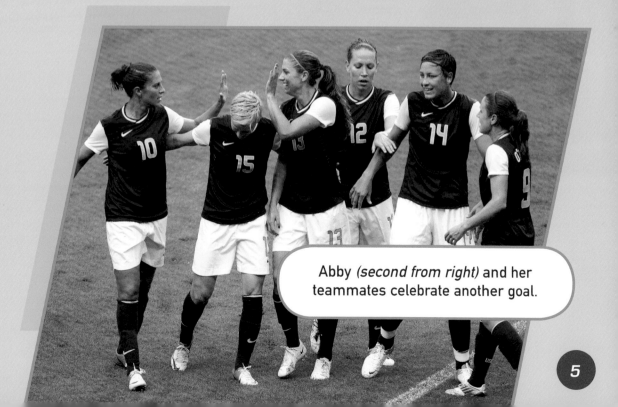

Abby *(second from right)* and her teammates celebrate another goal.

The **referee** called a **penalty** a few minutes after Canada's third goal. She said that a Canadian player had touched the ball with her arm. Soccer rules don't allow a player to touch the ball with her arms or hands. The referee gave Team USA a **penalty kick**.

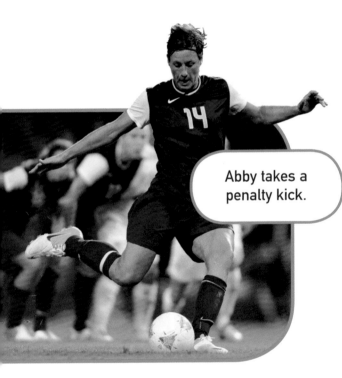

Abby takes a penalty kick.

The US team wanted their best scorer to take the kick. They chose Abby.

Abby set the ball on the grass and stepped back. She looked from the ball to the goal. When the referee blew her whistle, Abby stepped forward and launched the ball.

It raced across the grass. The ball bounced off the left **goal post** and into the net! The game was tied, 3–3.

After 90 minutes, the match was still tied. The game went into **extra time**. Neither team could score in the 30 minutes of extra time. Then, in the

Most soccer matches have two halves of 45 minutes each. If the match is tied after the second half, the teams play a 30-minute extra-time period.

third minute of **injury time**, the match finally ended. Abby's teammate Alex Morgan knocked a **header** into the back of the net. Team USA would have a chance to win the gold medal.

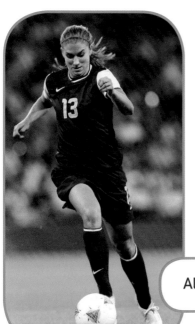

Alex Morgan drives the ball down the field.

US coach Pia Sundhage knew the gold medal match a few days later would be hard. But she also knew her team would fight for the win. "The team refuses to lose," Sundhage said.

Coach Sundhage trains her team to go for the gold medal.

Abby's mom *(left)* shares her excitement over a US victory.

GROWING UP SPORTY

Becoming one of the top athletes in a sport isn't easy. It takes years of work and practice. The best athletes often get a lot of support from their families as they grow up and learn their sport. Abby had more support than most.

Pittsford is a suburb of Rochester, New York. It lies close to Lake Ontario.

Mary Abigail Wambach was born on June 2, 1980, in Pittsford, New York. Her parents, Judy and Peter, called her Abby. Abby has two older sisters, Beth and Laura. She also has four older brothers, Andy, Peter, Matthew, and Patrick.

The Wambachs are an athletic family. "I played every sport that my brothers and sisters played," Abby said. She and her brothers and sisters had a lot of fun at home. "We had a pool in

Abby likes to spend time outside. Biking and camping are two of her favorite activities.

our backyard, so I swam a bunch," Abby said.

Abby's siblings didn't go easy on her just because she was younger. "My brothers never let me win, although they would probably beg to differ," she said. Growing up in a house full of older athletes made Abby better. She always worked hard to keep up.

Abby joined her first youth team at the age of four. She showed a special talent for soccer. She played on the girls' team and scored 27 goals in her first three games.

Abby first played soccer on a youth team for both boys and girls. The kids in this photo also play youth soccer.

Her parents and coaches decided to move her to the boys' team. Abby felt right at home. She was used to playing against her brothers.

Abby played many different sports growing up. But by the time she reached high school, it was time to focus on one or two. She chose soccer and basketball.

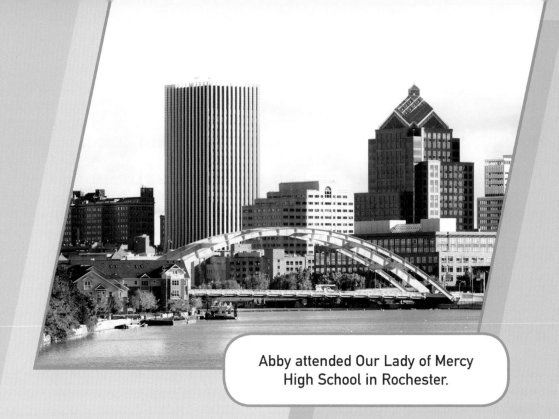

Abby attended Our Lady of Mercy
High School in Rochester.

GATOR GIRL

Abby was a standout basketball player in high
school. She made her school's **varsity** team as
a freshman in 1994. Freshman athletes rarely
make their school's top team. Abby played
for the varsity team during all four years of
high school.

Abby enjoyed playing basketball. But she put her heart into soccer. She proved early in high school that she had a chance to be a great soccer player. But Abby didn't realize at the time just how good she could be. "She had no idea the potential she had," said her high school coach.

Abby scored 142 goals in her four-year high school career. This is an incredible number of goals for a soccer player. She racked up 34 goals as a senior in 1997 and won a bunch of awards. The biggest was the National High School Player of the Year award. Later that year, Abby had to decide on her next move.

The University of North Carolina women's soccer team is often the best in the country. They've won the national championship an incredible 21 times since 1982.

The University of Florida (*below*) is in Gainesville, Florida.

As the best female high school soccer player in the country, Abby could choose between many different colleges. The University of North Carolina had one of the best women's soccer teams in the country at the time. They wanted Abby. But she had her eye on another top soccer school. She chose to go to the University of Florida.

Abby started 26 games for the Florida Gators as a freshman in 1998. She finished second on the team with 19 goals. She also had 12 **assists**.

Abby (*right*) fights for the ball in a game against the University of Kentucky Wildcats.

Even better, the Gators made it all the way to the National Collegiate Athletic Association (NCAA) championship game.

They faced the North Carolina Tar Heels, the team that had wanted Abby before she chose Florida. The Tar Heels had beaten the Gators earlier in the year, 2–1. This time, Florida came out on top, 1–0. Abby and her teammates were national champions!

Abby became team captain of the Gators during her senior year at the University of Florida.

GOING PRO

Abby played for the Gators from 1998 to 2001. In that time, she scored 96 goals and added 50 assists. She is still Florida's all-time leader in goals and assists. But the Gators couldn't get back to the NCAA championship game after winning it in 1998.

When Abby began her college career, she didn't plan to keep playing soccer after school. But in 2001, the Women's United Soccer Association (WUSA) started play. WUSA was the world's first women's soccer league in which every player was paid. Abby decided to join the league. The Washington Freedom chose her with the second pick

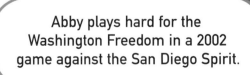

Abby plays hard for the Washington Freedom in a 2002 game against the San Diego Spirit.

Abby kicks the ball in a 2003 match against the Atlanta Beat.

during the 2002 **draft**. The team's home was near Washington, DC.

Abby had a great season in 2002. The WUSA named her Rookie of the Year. The 2003 season was even better. The Freedom made it to the WUSA championship game. They faced the Atlanta Beat. Abby scored early in the match with a header. Then Atlanta scored.

With the match tied 1–1, the championship game headed into extra time. Six minutes later, Abby scored her second goal of the match.

Abby holds the Founders Cup after winning the WUSA championship.

The Freedom became WUSA champions! Abby was named Most Valuable Player (MVP) of the game. "It's the greatest feeling that I've had in my soccer career," she said.

Abby and her teammates wouldn't get the chance to repeat their championship. WUSA was losing money. The league went out of business after the 2003 season. Abby turned her focus to the 2004 Olympic Games in Athens, Greece.

The US Women's National Team was the best in the world in 2004. They cruised through the Olympics. They were favored to win the gold medal match against Brazil. But the score was tied after regular time.

Heather O'Reilly (*left*) hugs Abby after their team's gold medal win against Brazil.

Then, in the 112th minute, Abby scored the game-winning goal. When time ran out, Abby and her teammates met on the field for a huge hug. They were gold medal winners!

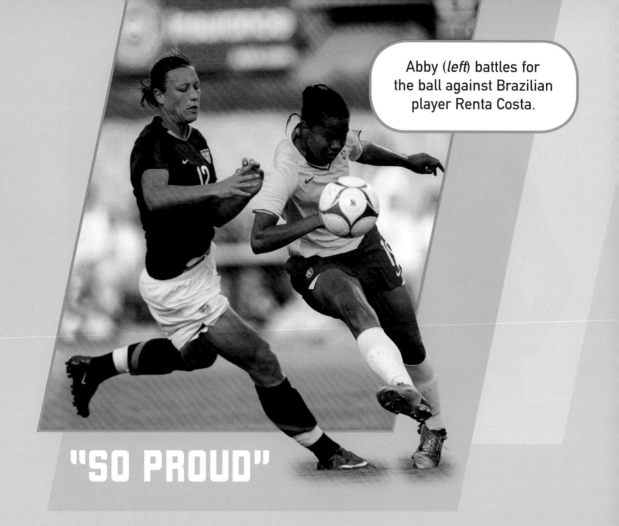

Abby (*left*) battles for the ball against Brazilian player Renta Costa.

"SO PROUD"

Abby kept playing for the US Women's National Team after the Olympics. She had become one of the best scorers in the world. But disaster struck in the last match before the 2008 Olympics in Beijing, China. Abby crashed into a Brazilian player.

Abby (*left*) posed for Olympic photos with her 2008 teammates before a leg injury took her out of the competition.

The US star broke two bones in her leg. She wouldn't play soccer again for more than a year.

Abby knew that her team could win without her. "I'm only one player, and you can never win a championship with just one player," she said. Abby was right. Team USA took home the gold medal.

Abby leaps high above Japanese players in the final match of the 2011 World Cup.

The next big event for the US Women's National Team was the 2011 World Cup in Frankfurt, Germany. They won game after game until they faced Japan in the final match. It was tied 2–2 after regular time. Then Abby scored with a header in extra time. It was her fourth goal of the **tournament**.

Japan tied the score again. The game went to a **penalty shootout**. When Abby's turn came, she scored. But Japan won the shootout, 3–1.

Megan Rapinoe (*left*) plays to win against Japan in the 2012 Olympics.

Abby was upset to come up short in the World Cup. But she didn't have time to dwell on the loss. She had to get ready for the 2012 Olympics. After beating Canada in the semifinal, Team USA would have to take down Japan for the gold medal. Abby and her teammates wanted revenge after losing to

Japan in the World Cup. "They snatched our dream last summer," said US player Megan Rapinoe.

This time, the US women beat Japan, 2–1. Abby knelt on the field and cried before celebrating with her teammates.

Team USA celebrates with a group hug after defeating Japan for the gold medal.

In June of 2013, Abby broke Mia Hamm's world record for international goals. Hamm's previous record was 159 international goals scored.

US fans were thrilled. Even President Barack Obama was happy for the team. "Congrats to the U.S. women's soccer team for a third straight Olympic gold," the president wrote on Twitter. "So proud."

With Abby at the top of her game, Team USA can look forward to many proud moments.

Abby (*right*) gets a Gatorade bath after breaking the international goal-scoring record.

Selected Career Highlights

2012 Helped Team USA win gold medal at Olympic Games

2011 Helped Team USA finish second in the World Cup

2009 Scored 100th goal as a member of Team USA

2008 Missed Olympic Games after breaking leg

2007 Scored six goals in six World Cup games

2004 Scored game-winning goal in gold medal match at Olympic Games
Named US Soccer's Female Athlete of the Year for the second time

2003 Won WUSA championship with the Washington Freedom
Named US Soccer's Female Athlete of the Year

2002 Chosen with the second pick in WUSA draft
Named WUSA Rookie of the Year

2001 Named Southeastern Conference Player of the Year for the second time
Named Southeastern Conference Tournament MVP for the second time
Named to NCAA Division I Women's All-America Team for the fourth time

2000 Named Southeastern Conference Player of the Year
Named Southeastern Conference Tournament MVP
Named to NCAA Division I Women's All-America Team for the third time

1999 Named to NCAA Division I Women's All-America Team for the second time

1998 Named to NCAA Division I Women's All-America Team

1997 Named female High School Player of the Year for soccer

Glossary

assists: passes to teammates that help score goals

draft: a yearly event in which teams pick new players

extra time: time added to the end of a soccer match if the score is tied

goal post: one of the two posts on either side of a soccer goal

header: passing or shooting the ball by bouncing it off one's head

injury time: time added to the end of a soccer match to make up for the time lost by player injuries

penalty: punishment for breaking a rule

penalty kick: a free kick at the goal

penalty shootout: a way to decide the winner of a match. Each team takes turns taking penalty kicks until a winner is decided.

referee: a person who watches a match to make sure the rules are followed

semifinal: the next-to-last match in a tournament

tournament: a set of games held to decide the best team

varsity: the top team at a school

Further Reading & Websites

Eason, Sarah, and Paul Mason. *Street Soccer*. Minneapolis: Lerner Publications Company, 2012.

Savage, Jeff. *David Beckham*. Minneapolis: Lerner Publications Company, 2013.

Stewart, Mark, and Mike Kennedy. *Goal! The Fire and Fury of Soccer's Greatest Moment*. Minneapolis: Millbrook Press, 2010.

Abby Wambach
http://www.abbywambach.com/wambach/index
Abby's official website has all kinds of information about one of the best female soccer players in the world.

Sports Illustrated Kids
http://www.sikids.com
The *Sports Illustrated Kids* website covers all sports, including soccer.

US Women—US Soccer
http://www.ussoccer.com/teams/us-women.aspx
The official website of the US Women's National Team has news, schedules, profiles of your favorite soccer stars, and much more.

Index

Photo Acknowledgments

The images in this book are used with the permission of: AP Photo/Jon Super, p. 4; © Phil Oldman/Colorsport/CORBIS, p. 5; © John Todd/ISI/CORBIS, p. 6, 29; © Martin Bernetti/AFP/Getty Images, p. 7; © Robin Parker/CORBIS, p. 8; AP Photo/ Julio Cortez, p. 9; © Photoquest/Dreamstime.com, p. 10; © Robert Pernell/ Dreamstime.com, p. 11; © Photoquest/Dreamstime.com, p. 13; © Irina Silayeva/ Dreamstime.com, p. 15; © Alan Campbell , pp. 16, 17; Isaac Menashe/Icon SMI738/Newscom, p. 18; © Paul J. Sutton/Duomo/CORBIS, p. 19; © Donald Miralle/ Getty Images, p. 20; REUTERS/Jeff J Mitchell, p. 21; Derrick Tuskan/Icon SMI 125/ Newscom, p. 23; Brian Kersey/UPI/Newscom, p. 24; © Tony QuinnIcon SMI/ CORBIS, p. 25; Kyodo/Newscom, p. 26; Mohammad Khursheed/Newscom, p. 27; © Al Bello/Getty Images, p. 28.

Front cover: Keith Nordstrom/AI Wire/Newscom.

Main body text set in Caecilia LT Std 55 Roman 16/28.
Typeface provided by Adobe Systems.